Published by Barbour Publishing, Inc., P.O. Box 719, Uhrichsville, Ohio 44683
http://www.barbourbooks.com

Member of the
Evangelical Christian
Publishers Association

Printed in China.

I'm Praying for You

Ellyn Sanna

BARBOUR
PUBLISHING, INC.

We give thanks to God
and the Father of our Lord Jesus Christ,
praying always for you.

4–I'M PRAYING FOR YOU

I'm praying that you will. . .

    know God's peace.
    feel God's love.
    trust in God's hope.
    experience God's joy.
    rest in God's patience.

I'M PRAYING FOR YOU—5

"*All* I can do is pray," I find myself saying, as though that weren't very much at all. But the truth is, prayer is the *most* I can do. Prayer unites me with God's creative power; prayer moves mountains and shapes our world for God.

So today, please know my prayers are with you. I know God will move the mountains in your life.

1

I'm praying that you will know God's peace. . . .

Let the peace that comes from Christ
rule in your hearts. . . .

COLOSSIANS 3:15 NLT

$\mathcal{L}\!\mathit{et}$ the ways of childish confidence and freedom from care. . .
teach you what should be your ways with God; and, leaving
yourself in His hands, learn to be literally "careful for nothing";
and you shall find it to be a fact that the peace of God, which
passeth all understanding, shall keep (as with a garrison) your
heart and mind through Christ Jesus.

HANNAH WHITALL SMITH

It is in forgetfulness of self that we find peace.

LILIAN WHITING

*Even in the low points,
my heart always runs to the Father
and finds peace only in Him.*

GWEN SHAMBLIN

Let the matchless love of God
sweep away your doubts and fears.
You already have God's attention,
and you will never lose it.

JONI EARECKSON TADA

If peace be in the heart, the wildest winter storm
is full of solemn beauty.

C. F. RICHARDSON

I am not afraid of storms,
for I am learning how to sail my ship.

LOUISA MAY ALCOTT

The stronger the winds, the deeper the roots,
and the longer the winds,
the more beautiful the tree.

CHARLES R. SWINDOLL

Through all life's storms, may you know that your roots are sunk deep in God. Although stormy winds rip through your leaves, you will not be shaken. Do not be afraid of the dark clouds or the wild gales; rely on your sure foundation in God.

I'm praying that His peace will make you strong.

When life seems overwhelming,

   when nothing seems to make any sense,

     when the pain seems too great to bear,

       when you have only questions and no answers,

please know my prayers are with you. May God's peace wrap
'round your heart.

2

I'm praying that you will feel God's love. . . .

Keep yourselves in God's love.

JUDE 21 NIV

"God so loved the world that he gave"—no end,
no time limit, no measure, no calculation.
His giving could only be called a reckless abandonment of love.

HELEN ROSEVEARE

The love of God accomplishes
all things quietly and completely;
it is not anxious or uncertain.

LILIAN WHITING

Set your thoughts, not on the storm,
but on the Love that rules the storm.

MRS. CHARLES E. COWMAN

God's love toward me is kind.
God's love toward me is patient.
God's love toward me is not provoked.
God's love toward me does not take
into account a wrong suffered.
God's love toward me would bear all things,
believe all things, hope all things, endure all things.
God's love toward me would never fail.

NEY BAILEY (BASED ON 1 CORINTHIANS 13)

I see Thy mercy, limitless as space,
I see Thy love and feel Thy close embrace;
And though Thy presence fills the universe,
Yet close as hands and heart Thou art to me.

OLGA J. WEISS

I have loved you with an everlasting love;
therefore I have continued my faithfulness to you.

JEREMIAH 31:3 NRSV

*You'll never, ever, be alone again.
You are bone of His bone—
an indispensable member of His body.*

KAY ARTHUR

Sometimes circumstances seem to say that God's love has disappeared—but His love is with you, no matter what. There is nowhere you can go where you will be separated from His concern for you; His love surrounds you even in the darkest night, the coldest winter storm.

I'm praying that you will feel His arms of love holding you tight against His heart.

3

I'm praying that you will trust in God's hope. . . .

There is surely a future hope for you,
and your hope will not be cut off.

PROVERBS 23:18 NIV

Sometimes life seems impossible. No matter where you look, you see only dark skies and despair. But remember—the clouds only hide the sun; they do not put it out. And no matter how terrible events seem, God's grace shines on undimmed. Your view may be blocked by life's looming obstacles—but against all odds, God's love is still aflame. And nothing, not all the forces of evil, can extinguish this amazing light.

I'm praying that you'll never give up hope.

Even in the midst of winter, even in the midst of the storm,
the sun is still there. . . . Spring will come!
The clouds cannot stay forever.

GLORIA GAITHER

*Hope does not disappoint us, because God
has poured out his love into our hearts by
the Holy Spirit, whom he has given us.*

ROMANS 5:5 NIV

I pray also that the eyes of your heart
may be enlightened in order that you
may know the hope to which he has called you,
the riches of his glorious inheritance. . . ,
and his incomparably great power for us who believe.

EPHESIANS 1:18–19 NIV

Since we have so often experienced our deserts to be turned into the garden of the Lord, and have found fir trees and myrtle trees coming up where we thought there were only thorns and briers, the marvelous thing is that we should ever let ourselves be so utterly cast down and overwhelmed when fresh trouble comes.

HANNAH WHITALL SMITH

Faith looks up and sails on,
by God's great Sun,
not seeing one shoreline or earthly lighthouse
or path upon the way.
Often it seems to lead into utter uncertainty
and even darkness and disaster;
but He opens the way
and often makes midnight hours the very gates of day.
Let us go forth this day, not knowing, but trusting.

MRS. CHARLES E. COWMAN

Hope is like the sun, which, as we journey toward it, casts the shadow of our burden behind us.

SAMUEL SMILES

Find rest, O my soul,
in God alone; my hope comes from him.

PSALM 62:5 NIV

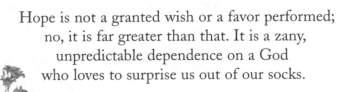

Hope is not a granted wish or a favor performed; no, it is far greater than that. It is a zany, unpredictable dependence on a God who loves to surprise us out of our socks.

MAX LUCADO

Hope means to keep living amid desperation
and to keep humming in the darkness.

HENRI J. NOUWEN

*Delicate threads of hope, patiently woven,
become the strong fabric of our faith.*

JANET L. WEAVER

Hope does not necessarily take the form
of excessive confidence; rather,
it involves the simple willingness
to take the next step.

STANLEY HAUERWAS

I know how hard things are right now—but I'm praying you will not give in to despair. God works for good through even the most difficult events. You may not see His hand at work—but when you look back, you will see His fingerprints everywhere.

Hope in Him. He will not disappoint you.

4

I'm praying that you will experience God's joy. . . .

I will turn their mourning into gladness;
I will give them comfort
and joy instead of sorrow.

JEREMIAH 31:13 NIV

Happiness is usually caused by circumstances. . . .
Supernatural joy, however, enables us to experience a deeper joy.

SUSAN ALEXANDER YATES

You may feel as though you have little reason to be happy. But God's joy reaches far deeper than mere happiness, and it is always present, even when your heart is aching. God's joy rests on the assurance that He is working in even the most painful times; because of Jesus, you are guaranteed a happy ending to your story.

I'm praying that you will feel the joy of God even now.

Just as the simple presence of the mother makes the child's joy, so does the simple fact of God's presence with us make our joy.

HANNAH WHITALL SMITH

No distress need cramp us, crowd us into ourselves,
or make us smaller and poorer in anything that matters.
Largeness, like the largeness of the sea, is His gift to us.
We shall not be flattened by pressure, but enlarged.
In the narrow ways of pain or temptation
He will make wide room for us.

AMY CARMICHAEL

*Thou hast enlarged me
when I was in distress.*

PSALM 4:1 KJV

They that wait upon the LORD shall renew their strength.
They shall mount up with wings like eagles;
they shall run and not be weary;
they shall walk and shall not faint.

ISAIAH 40:31 TLB

The spirit of happiness is sheer miracle.
It is the gift of the happy God.

AMY CARMICHAEL

We look at our burdens and heavy loads
and shrink from them; but as we lift them
and bind them about our hearts,
they become wings; and on them
we rise and soar toward God.

MRS. CHARLES E. COWMAN

You can come out of the furnace of trouble two ways:
if you let it consume you, you come out a cinder;
but there is a kind of metal which refuses to be consumed
and comes out a star.

JEAN CHURCH

When life threatens to consume you, remember—God's grace will keep you safe. I am praying that one day, when this time is over, you will shine like a star for all to see.

And in the meantime, enjoy the little things of life. Taste the small blessings God sprinkles through your days. Open your heart to God's joy.

Sing, O heavens! Be joyful, O earth!
And break out in singing, O mountains!
For the LORD has comforted His people,
And will have mercy on His afflicted.

ISAIAH 49:13 NKJV

Joyful, joyful, we adore Thee,
God of glory, Lord of love;
Hearts unfold like flowers before Thee,
Opening to the sun above.
Melt the clouds of sin and sadness,
Drive the dark of doubt away;
Giver of immortal gladness,
Fill us with the light of day.

HENRY VAN DYKE

Neglect, indifference, forgetfulness, ignorance, are all impossible to Him. He knows everything; He cares about everything; and He loves us! Surely this is enough for a "fullness of joy" beyond the power of words to express. . . .

HANNAH WHITALL SMITH

God is the highest good—good as nothing is but Himself. He is intrinsically happy; in fact, all good and all true happiness are to be found only in God, since they are essential to His nature. No one can be happy or experience any goodness unless God communicates His own glad goodness, and nothing pleases unless it is a vehicle for God.

JOHN BUNYAN

5

I'm praying that you will rest in God's patience. . . .

In your patience possess ye your souls.

LUKE 21:19 KJV

When life's pain seems overwhelming, when our strength is fading fast, and problems seem to pile up faster than solutions, we want God to come to our rescue *now*. We can't understand why He would delay, when we so obviously need His immediate attention.

But we *always* have His attention—and He is constantly, surely working through the circumstances of our lives. We can rest in Him, knowing that patiently, ceaselessly, He is weaving the dark fabrics of our life into a pattern of light and glory.

I'm praying that you will rest in Him. Allow His patience to give you strength and peace.

In waiting we begin to get in touch with the rhythms of life. . . .
They are the rhythms of God.
It is in the everyday and the commonplace
that we learn patience, acceptance, and contentment.

RICHARD J. FOSTER

Consider the farmers who eagerly look for the rains
in the fall and in the spring.
They patiently wait for the precious harvest to ripen.
You, too, must be patient.
And take courage. . . .

JAMES 5:7–8 NLT

. . .Noah exercised patience, waiting God's leisure
until the flood was taken away.
Grace, therefore, had seven more days' work to do,
and Noah had to wait that long before he received
any further news that the water was going down.
Waiting is hard work. Unfortunately, sometimes patience
is accomplished with so much feverish heat,
that every hour seems like seven until the trial is over
and the blessing can be possessed by the waiting soul.
Noah is not so different from us—and I'm sure the psalmist
was also just like us, for he said, "How long, O LORD,
until you restore me?" (Psalm 6:3 NLT).

JOHN BUNYAN

We all know what it feels like to be at rest.
And we all long for a more sane lifestyle
rather than being overwhelmed.
But are we willing to leave the press
long enough to lie down in the soothing green pastures
and to be led by the still waters of His provision?

PATSY CLAIRMONT

He maketh me to lie down in green pastures:
he leadeth me beside the still waters.

PSALM 23:2 KJV

Patience takes away all wobbling. . . .
God's foundations are steady.

MRS. CHARLES E. COWMAN

Sometime life feels pretty uncertain.
But I'm praying that no matter how wobbly your heart feels,
you will be able to relax. . .rest. . .
and allow God's patience to make you strong.

Come to Me,
all you who labor
and are heavy laden,
and I will give you rest.

MATTHEW 11:28 NKJV